SUPER CITIES!

BALTIMORE

by Kathy MacMillan

arcadia®
CHILDREN'S BOOKS

Published by Arcadia Children's Books
A Division of Arcadia Publishing
Charleston, SC
www.arcadiapublishing.com

Super Cities is a trademark of Arcadia Publishing, Inc.

First published 2023

Manufactured in the United States of America.

ISBN 978-1-4671-9898-1

Library of Congress Control Number: 2022950473

Notice: The information in this book is true and complete to the best of our knowledge. It is offered without guarantee on the part of the author or Arcadia Publishing. The author and Arcadia Publishing disclaim all liability in connection with the use of this book.

Produced by Shoreline Publishing Group LLC
Santa Barbara, California
Designer: Patty Kelley
Production: Steve Solution

Contents

Welcome to Baltimore.................4

Baltimore: Map It!...................6

Naming Baltimore...................8

The Inner Harbor...................10

History: Early Days.................12

History: Colonial and
  Revolutionary Times.......14

History: Baltimore at War.........16

History: Immigrants and Innovation 18

History: The 20th Century.........20

History: Civil Rights Milestones.....22

People of the Past.................24

On the Streets of Baltimore........26

Religious Traditions...............28

Things to See.....................30

Baltimore's Musical Heritage.......38

Seasons in the City...............40

Getting Around Baltimore.........42

Museums: Go See 'Em!............44

Outdoor Art......................48

Art Museums.....................50

Charm City Creatives..............52

How to Speak Baltimore...........54

Hon Culture.....................56

Baltimore: It's Weird!.............58

Famous People Today.............60

What People Do in Baltimore......62

Giving Back and Doing Good.......64

Eat the Baltimore Way............66

All About Crabs!!..................68

Oriole Park at Camden Yards......70

Go, Baltimore Sports.............72

College Town....................76

It's Alive: Animals in Baltimore......78

We Saw It at the Zoo.............80

Spooky Sites....................82

Baltimore Firsts..................84

Not Far Away....................86

Sister Cities Around the World......90

Find Out More......................92

Index.............................94

WELCOME TO Baltimore!

Baltimore, Maryland

A lot of Baltimore is in the middle of two things. Located in Maryland, it's officially in the American South, but it's probably more tied to the North. The city's rich history has seen it grow from a colonial-era boomtown to a key site for both the Underground Railroad and the Civil War. More recent years have seen the city transformed into one of the most innovative on the East Coast.

On the streets of Baltimore, you'll see stately historical monuments like the Washington Monument—no, *not* the one you're thinking of. Baltimore's 178-foot tower was built in 1829,

19 years *before* the famous version in Washington DC. But you'll also see quirky modern art like the 51-foot tall, 14-ton aluminum Male/Female sculpture that looms over Pennsylvania Station.

Since the mid-twentieth century, Baltimore has jazzed up its downtown area to become a center of business and tourism. When you visit Baltimore, you'll meet "Hons," watch Orioles that don't fly, and eat crabs and scrapple! Baltimore has been called a lot of things: quirky, eccentric, scary, an underdog. But one thing is certain: it's anything but boring!

BALTIMORE: Map It!

Baltimore, Maryland, is located roughly in the center of the East Coast of the United States. The city sits at the mouth of the Patapsco River, which flows into the Chesapeake Bay. The bay then connects to the Atlantic Ocean to the east. The Appalachian Mountains are to the west of the city. Baltimore City separated from Baltimore County in 1851. It is the only city in Maryland that functions outside of a county government.

Baltimore, Maryland

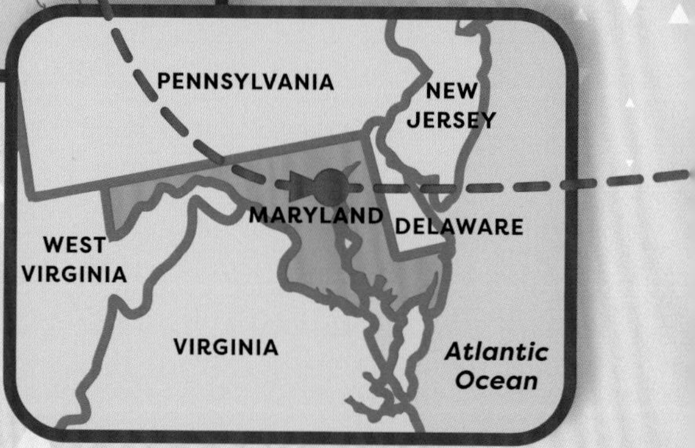

PENNSYLVANIA

NEW JERSEY

WEST VIRGINIA

MARYLAND DELAWARE

VIRGINIA

Atlantic Ocean

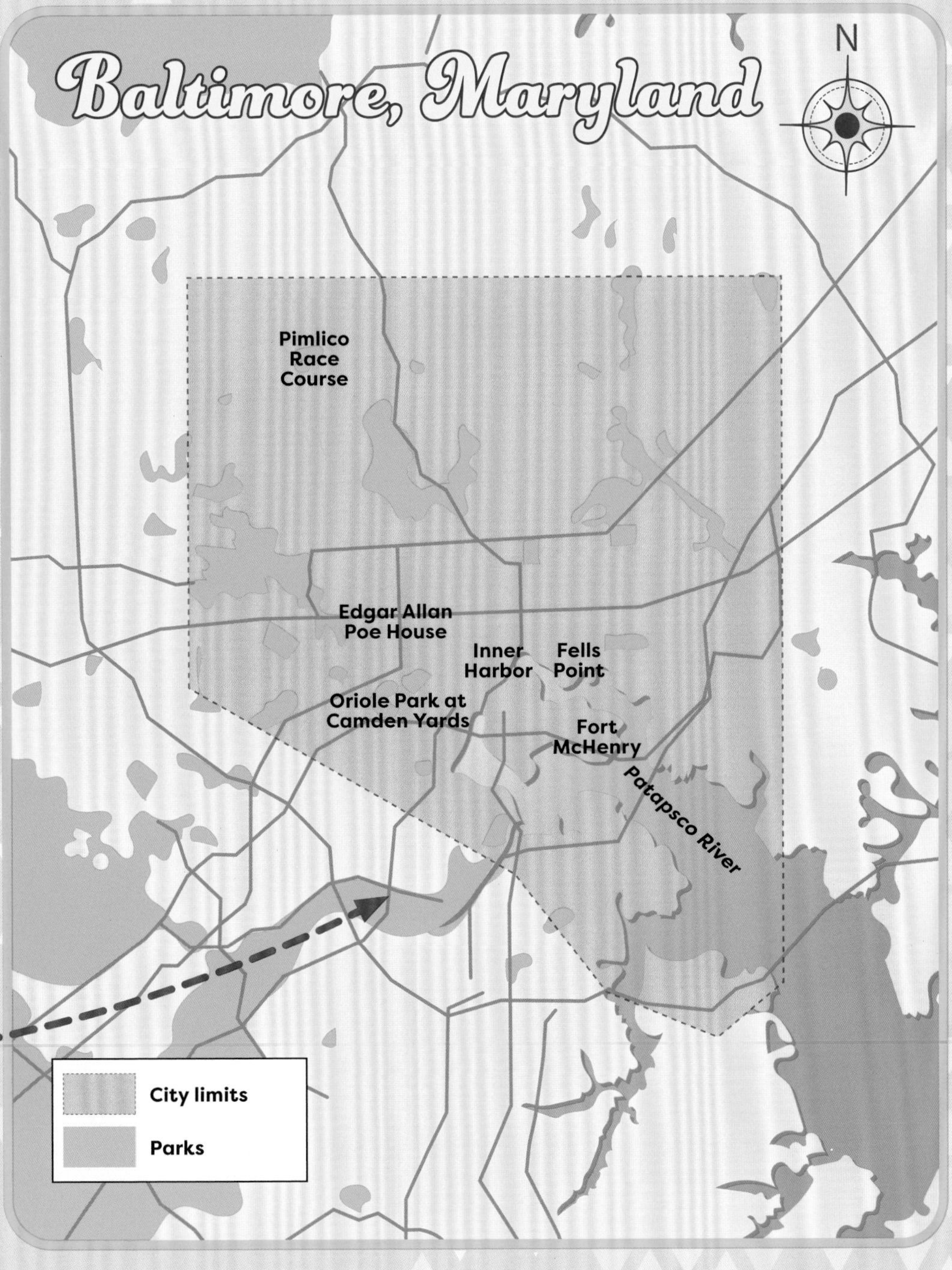

Baltimore, Maryland

N

Pimlico
Race
Course

Edgar Allan
Poe House

Inner
Harbor

Fells
Point

Oriole Park at
Camden Yards

Fort
McHenry

Patapsco River

City limits

Parks

NAMING BALTIMORE

Sir George Calvert, a member of the British nobility in Ireland, was granted the title Lord Baltimore in 1625. The word "Baltimore" is an English adaptation of the Irish phrase *baile an thí mhóir e* ("town of the big house"). The Calvert family, like many Roman Catholics in Great Britain in the mid-1600s, faced prejudice from followers of the Church of England. George Calvert wanted to establish a colony in America based on religious toleration (which means letting people practice whatever faith they want). Britain's King Charles I granted him a royal charter to settle the area north of Virginia.

George Calvert

King Charles

Unfortunately, George Calvert died before the charter was signed. So the colony of Maryland was established by his son, Cecil Calvert, the second Lord Baltimore. Following his father's wishes, Cecil created a colony where Christians of any denomination could freely practice their religion. Though he never actually got to visit Maryland himself, Cecil governed from his home in England for 42 years until his death in 1675. Cecil is the official namesake of the city of Baltimore. Other areas in Maryland are also named in his honor, including Calvert County and Cecil County.

Cecil Calvert

Maryland's Flag

The Maryland state flag features two coats of arms. The gold and black bars are from the Calvert family, while the red and white cross design is from the Crossland family, from which came George Calvert's mother, Alice. Various versions of the flag were used in the state's early history. During the Civil War, many Confederate sympathizers used the red and white Crossland design only, to set themselves apart from Maryland's Union sympathizers. In the 1880s, lawmakers settled on the combination design to symbolize Marylanders coming together after the Civil War. It became the official state flag in 1904. Many Marylanders love their bold and unique flag. You'll find them wearing the state flag design on everything from bikinis and shorts to masks and neckties!

Maryland's
state flower, the
Black-eyed Susan

The Inner Harbor

Once home to steel mills and shipyards, the Inner Harbor is now Baltimore's top tourist destination. It's full of shops, restaurants, and museums. Here are just some of the highlights of this busy area.

Seven-Foot Knoll Lighthouse
Most lighthouses are very tall, to be seen from far away. From 1856 to 1948, this seven-foot lighthouse helped ships navigate Baltimore's harbor. Today, it's a small museum.

Historic Ships in Baltimore

Learn about life at sea as you explore the decks of the USS *Constellation*, built in 1854 as the US Navy's final sail-only warship. Also, check out the USS *Torsk*, a World War II submarine.

The National Aquarium

Visit with animal species from all over the world, from Atlantic puffins to blacktip reef sharks to golden lion tamarins, at one of the country's top aquariums. Be sure to visit the Living Seashore, where you'll get to pet a stingray.

Chessie Dragon Paddle Boat

Chessie is the name of a "sea monster" that supposedly lives in the Chesapeake Bay. In honor of the popular legend, you can ride paddle boats in the harbor designed to look like what some artists think Chessie might look like. If you see her, though... steer the other way!

HISTORY: Early Days

The first inhabitants of the Chesapeake Bay region arrived more than 10,000 years ago. They came to hunt wildlife in the forests and fish the waterways. By 1,000 BCE, Maryland was home to about 40 different groups of Indigenous peoples.

Woodland People: This group became the dominant Indigenous people in the area. The Chesapeake Bay provided them with plenty of oysters, herring, and bass. The nearby freshwater marshes were full of cattails and other edible plants. They moved inland to create farming villages, where they grew corn, peas, tobacco, and other crops. But they maintained hunting and fishing camps near the bay.

Meet the Locals!: Later, the Paskestikweya (Pist-ka-tah-wah) tribe (also known as Piscataway) lived on the land that is now known as Baltimore. Like most of the tribes in the area, they spoke the Algonquian language. These tribes were linked by trade networks that stretched as far away as today's New York and Ohio.

Trouble from Europe: After European settlers arrived, the population of Indigenous people declined. Many were killed by settlers. Many died of disease. Many left the area or were forced to relocate westward.

HISTORY: Colonial and Revolutionary Times

1649: The Province of Maryland passed the Maryland Toleration Act, the first law in America to refer to the "free exercise" of religion. Those words would later appear in the First Amendment to the US Constitution.

1729: Baltimore Town was established on sixty acres at the northern end of the Patapsco River. The town had only three streets. As the town grew, mills, bakeries, and tanneries sprang up. Baltimore's harbor made it ideal for shipping, with tobacco as the number one crop. Baltimore absorbed the local settlements of Jones's Town in 1745 and Fells Point in 1773.

1758: Dr. John Stevenson, who believed that Baltimore's harbor had the potential for more than just tobacco trade, shipped 1,000 bushels of wheat to New York. Others quickly followed, building mills along nearby streams. The mills ground the wheat into flour to sell to other colonies and the world. Ships were soon leaving Baltimore's harbor with flour for Great Britain and the Caribbean.

1776: The Continental Congress met in Philadelphia, Pennsylvania, to adopt the Declaration of Independence, officially separating the colonies from Great Britain. Four of its signers were from Maryland. Later in the year, with British troops advancing, the Continental Congress moved from Philadelphia to Baltimore. From December 20, 1776 to February 27, 1777, they met in the three-story Baltimore home of Henry Fite.

1790: The census that year showed that enslaved Black people outnumbered free Black people two to one. Slave traders from Virginia, Kentucky, and other southern states built slave pens right by the port. Thousands of African people who had been taken from their homes came through the Port of Baltimore before being sent south.

1806: The National Road was built from the Ohio River to Cumberland, Maryland (about 140 miles west of Baltimore). Baltimore business owners quickly constructed a system of turnpikes to connect Baltimore to the National Road, allowing for easier trade with the farmlands of the Ohio Valley.

THE NATIONAL ROAD (1850)

1812: The United States was once again at war with England, this time over trade disputes. Baltimore was producing the fastest, easiest to maneuver ships in the world. In these "Baltimore Clippers," privateers (ships hired by the US to fight the British) captured 25 percent of the British ships taken during the war.

1814: In August, British troops captured Washington, DC. Their next target was nearby Baltimore—and the city's main defense of Fort McHenry, a star-shaped fort manned by 1,000 soldiers. On September 13, the British Navy pummeled Fort McHenry (left) with bombs for 25 hours. An American lawyer named Francis Scott Key (top left) watched the battle from a ship in the harbor. When he raised his spyglass in the morning light, he was astonished to see the American flag still waving proudly over Fort McHenry. The British had lost the Battle of Baltimore. Key wrote a poem about the battle, using a popular melody of the time. The song became "The Star-Spangled Banner." It was treated as the national anthem of the US long before Congress made it official in 1931.

1827: The Baltimore and Ohio Railroad, America's first commercial railroad, was founded. It carried both passengers and freight, and connected Baltimore to the West. By the 1870s, it had expanded to reach Chicago, Illinois, and St. Louis, Missouri.

1830s: From the 1830s to the end of the Civil War in 1865, the Underground Railroad helped between 40,000 to 100,000 enslaved people escape to freedom. It was not an actual railroad, but a secret network of people who led escapees from one hiding place to another until they arrived in the north. Many of Baltimore's Quakers participated in the Underground Railroad, hiding people at the Old Town Friends Meeting House (below) and other spots around the harbor.

HISTORY: Immigrants and More War

1850: About two million immigrants came through the Port of Baltimore between 1850 and 1900, making it second only to Ellis Island, New York, as a port of entry. German, Irish, Scottish, French, Haitian, Eastern European, Greek, and Italian immigrants came in waves over the years. Each group found a home in Baltimore's diverse neighborhoods.

1861: As the Civil War broke out, Baltimoreans were divided over whether to support the Union or the Confederacy. The first land battle of the Civil War took place in Baltimore in April 1861. As the Union's 6th Massachusetts Infantry Regiment came through town on their way to Washington, DC, a mob of Confederate supporters attacked. Four soldiers and 13 civilians died in what came to be known as the Pratt Street Riot.

1862: On September 17, the Civil War's bloodiest day of battle took place at Antietam Creek, about 75 miles west of Baltimore. More than 25,000 Union and Confederate soldiers were killed or wounded in the battle. Thousands of wounded soldiers fled to Baltimore and took shelter in civilian homes and makeshift hospitals. The war ended in 1865 with the Union winning.

1880s: Baltimore's industries were going strong. The city was the largest supplier of canned fruits and vegetables in the country, and the largest supplier of oysters in the world. Sparrow's Point would soon become home to one of the world's largest steel and ship manufacturers. But another big industry might surprise you—Baltimore's factories produced 280,000 tons of fertilizer each year! Where did they get it? Bird poop! Baltimore imported guano, which was bird droppings from islands on the Pacific Coast. Factories turned it all into food for plants.

1889: The first skyscraper in Baltimore, the Hammond Building, was built. Ten stories high, the structure had lower floors made of stone and brick. The building had 246 offices as well as shops on the ground floor.

Growing!

Baltimore's population just kept on growing, fueled by immigration, people looking for jobs in Baltimore's industries, and the city's status as a transportation hub. Check out these numbers:

1816: 46,000 people
1830: 80,000 people
1850: 169,000 people
1900: 508,957 people

1904: On February 7, the Great Baltimore Fire spread over 140 acres and destroyed 1,526 buildings and took more than a day to put out. Rebuilding Baltimore's downtown would take ten years.

1917: World War I increased the demand for weapons, ships, and other goods, and people poured into Baltimore from the southern states to take jobs at factories. By 1920, Baltimore's population had risen to 733,826 and the city's land area had tripled in size.

1939–1946: Even before the United States officially entered World War II on December 7, 1941, Baltimore's economy was rebounding from the Great Depression of the 1930s. For the war, city factories churned out everything from gas masks to tanks to airplanes, all to support the war effort. Workers poured into the city looking for manufacturing jobs. By 1950, Baltimore was home to nearly 950,000 people.

1964: The city unveiled a master plan to revitalize the downtown area near the Inner Harbor with buildings, housing, parks, and a promenade. It would take about 20 years to complete, but the result was a success. Harborplace opened in 1980 and hosted more visitors than Disneyland in its first year.

1994: The Baltimore Orioles baseball team got a new home, Oriole Park at Camden Yards. The design merged features from classic ballparks of old with lots of new technology. It was an instant hit and inspired new ballparks around the country.

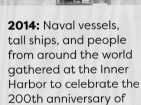

The National Aquarium

2014: Naval vessels, tall ships, and people from around the world gathered at the Inner Harbor to celebrate the 200th anniversary of the National Anthem.

2021: On December 25, the James Webb Space Telescope was launched. Operated by the Space Telescope Science Institute at Baltimore's Johns Hopkins University, it brings never-before-seen images of distant galaxies to astronomers worldwide.

HISTORY: Baltimore Civil Rights Milestones

1885: In June, six Baptist ministers founded the Mutual United Brotherhood of Liberty, an early civil rights organization. It focused on bringing legal challenges to fight discrimination, including bans on interracial marriage. By October, they had their first victory: Everett J. Waring became the first Black lawyer licensed to practice in Maryland.

Everett J. Waring

1933: The Baltimore branch of the National Association for the Advancement of Colored People (NAACP) had been established in 1914, but it gained new life when Dr. Lillie Carroll Jackson took over its leadership in 1933. As its leader for 35 years, she raised funds to support cases challenging discrimination in education, public accommodations, and employment. She died in 1975, and, at her request, her house became the Lillie Carroll Jackson Civil Rights Museum.

Dr. Lillie Carroll Jackson

1955: Five years before the famous Greensboro, North Carolina, lunch counter sit-ins, a group of activists from the Committee on Racial Equality (CORE) and Morgan State University protested racial segregation at Baltimore's downtown lunch counters. On January 20, 1955, Black activists sat down at counters at two Read's Drug Stores and refused to move. A few hours later, Read's announced the end of the segregation policy for all of its 300-plus lunch counters.

1968: Though schools were desegregated nationwide in 1954, long-standing patterns of discrimination meant that Baltimore's neighborhoods were still largely segregated. Many Black residents also lived in poverty. When Dr. Martin Luther King, Jr. was assassinated in Memphis, Tennessee, on April 4, 1968, Baltimore exploded into five days of unrest. Those days included everything from peaceful protests to looting and arson. National Guard troops were called in, and about one of every 75 Black residents of the city was arrested.

1960s: Racist real estate practices that limited where Black people could purchase homes led to Baltimore neighborhoods becoming segregated by race. Even today, the city can be mapped to what writer Dr. Lawrence T. Brown called "The White L and the Black Butterfly." In his 2021 book, he pointed out that more services are available in the L-shaped block of white neighborhoods than in the butterfly-shaped one of mostly Black neighborhoods.

2015: On April 12, a 25-year-old Black man named Freddie Gray was arrested by Baltimore City Police for possession of a knife—which was not illegal. Seven days later, Gray died from spinal cord injuries that happened during his arrest. Protests against police brutality exploded around the world. In Baltimore, some of those protests turned violent. Although six police officers were charged with Gray's murder, none were convicted.

People from the Past!

Meet some interesting people from Baltimore's past.

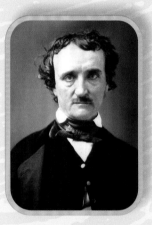

Edgar Allan Poe (1809–1849)
This famous American author is best known for his Gothic poem "The Raven." Poe was also a pioneer of horror, science fiction, and detective fiction. Many of his stories invite the reader to consider the evil that lurks within ordinary people. In an echo of the odd themes of his stories, Poe died under mysterious circumstances after being found drunk, wearing someone else's clothes, in a Baltimore tavern.

Frederick Douglass (1818–1895)
As a child enslaved in Baltimore, Frederick Douglass rebelled by teaching himself to read and write. In 1838, he escaped to freedom in the North and joined the abolitionist movement. He gave speeches and wrote about his experiences as an enslaved person, traveling the US and Europe as his fame grew. After the Civil War, he held several high-ranking government positions, including US Marshal for Washington DC.

Harriet Tubman (1820?–1913)

Born into slavery on Maryland's Eastern Shore, Harriet Tubman escaped to Philadelphia at age 27. Despite the risks, she returned to Maryland more than a dozen times to lead others to freedom via the secret routes of the Underground Railroad, earning the nickname "Moses." During the Civil War, she also served as a nurse and a Union spy.

Thurgood Marshall (1908–1993)

As chief of the NAACP Legal Defense and Educational Fund, Baltimore native Thurgood Marshall used the courts to fight discrimination. His most famous victory was *Brown v. Board of Education* in 1954, which declared segregation in public schools illegal. In 1967, Marshall became the first Black justice on the US Supreme Court.

Johnny Eck (1911–1991)

Born with no lower half of his body, Johnny Eck turned his sunny attitude and natural charisma into a successful career as a carnival and circus performer, doing everything from juggling to trapeze acts. He also appeared in several Hollywood films. In his later years, Eck returned to Baltimore and became a noted specialist in screen painting.

On the Streets of Baltimore

Here are some of the sights and places that are very unique to Baltimore.

Rowhouses: As immigrants arrived to work in Baltimore's factories and railroads, they needed places to live. Builders created rows of attached brick homes to provide affordable housing. Though many different styles of rowhouse would be built over the years, they remain popular to this day. Baltimore is home to more rowhouses than any other American city. Many have marble front stoops. Residents would scrub the marble weekly to keep it shining.

Painted Screens: In the windows of many rowhouses, you'll see colorful scenes of farmhouses, cityscapes, and more. These are painted screens, a Baltimore folk art tradition that started in 1913. A grocer named William Oktavec painted the screen doors of his shop with images of the food he sold inside. The idea caught on because the screens allowed for airflow while keeping people from seeing into their street-level windows. The Painted Screen Society of Baltimore, founded in 1985, maintains a schedule of classes and exhibitions to preserve this unique art.

Arabber Tradition: Peddlers with horse-drawn carts have sold fruits and vegetables on the streets of Baltimore since the city's earliest days, calling out what they were selling. These peddlers came to be called "Arabbers" (pronounced AY-rabbers), from a British slang phrase describing people who worked on the streets. You'll still see them on the streets of Baltimore today. Arabbers bring food to areas that don't have access to grocery stores. During the COVID-19 pandemic, they were critical in delivering food and information to city residents in lockdown. The Arabber Preservation Society was founded in 1994 to support the city's horse-cart vendors.

The Arabber's Call

Holler, holler, holler, till my throat get sore.
If it wasn't for the pretty girls, I wouldn't
*   have to holler no more.*
I say, Watermelon! Watermelon!
Get 'em red to the rind, lady.

Religious Traditions

The colony of Maryland was founded on the principle of religious freedom. Many different religious traditions thrive in Baltimore.

Methodist Church: On Christmas Eve, 1784, a meeting of 60 pastors was held at Lovely Lane Meeting House in Baltimore to organize the Methodist Episcopal Church in America. Today, Lovely Lane United Methodist Church is known as the Mother Church of American Methodism.

African Methodist Episcopal Church: In 1787, frustrated and angry with segregation in the church, a group of Black members left Lovely Lane. They went on to establish Bethel African Methodist Episcopal as an independent church. The church became a leader in pushing for social change, and remains a hub of the Black community in Baltimore.

Roman Catholic Church: In 1789, the first United States diocese of the Roman Catholic church was established in Baltimore, making it the seat of American Catholicism. Baltimore is also home to the first US cathedral, the Basilica of the National Shrine of the Assumption of the Blessed Virgin Mary, completed in 1821. The first American-born Catholic saint, St. Elizabeth Ann Seton, lived in Baltimore.

The Religious Society of Friends (Quakers): Since 1792, when the first Quaker Meetinghouse was established near Baltimore's harbor, Quakers have played an important role in the life of the city. Many Baltimore institutions, including Johns Hopkins University and Hospital, were founded by Quakers. Friends School of Baltimore, the city's first private school, was established in 1784. In 1821, the McKim Free School was established with money left by Quaker John McKim as the first school in Baltimore to provide a free education.

Unitarianism: In 1819, Rev. Dr. William Ellery Channing spoke at the First Independent Church of Baltimore, describing what would become the essence of the Unitarian Church: freedom, reason, tolerance, and social justice. His landmark "Baltimore Sermon" led to the founding of the Unitarian Church in 1825.

Judaism: In 1820, Baltimore had about 120 Jewish residents; by 1930, that number was 70,000. Baltimore became an important center of Orthodox Judaism with the opening of the Ner Israel Rabbinical College in 1933. The first American congregation founded on principles of Reformed Judaism, Har Sinai, was established in Baltimore in 1842.

Islam: The Islamic community joined Baltimore's religious traditions in 1943. Many Baltimore Muslims have been a part of the Nation of Islam, which combines traditional Islamic teachings with Black culture. Baltimore's first mosque was built in 1956 as Muhammad's Temple of Islam No. 6 of the Nation of Islam. In 1969, community members came together to establish the Islamic Society of Baltimore.

Islamic Society of Baltimore
Masjid Al-Rahmah

Community members dress as US soldiers from the War of 1812 at public shows.

Things to see in Baltimore

Fort McHenry

Built in 1803, Fort McHenry was an American military outpost, most famously in the War of 1812. The American victory in the 1814 Battle of Baltimore inspired the writing of "The Star-Spangled Banner." In 1939, the site was designated as a National Monument. Visit the fort to learn about the lives of the soldiers who served there, catch a living history program, or even try out a fife-and-drum camp!

Star-Spangled Banner Flag House

The flag that inspired Francis Scott Key to write "The Star-Spangled Banner" was enormous—30 x 42 feet. But where did it come from? Baltimore flagmaker Mary Pickersgill, along with several of her family members and indentured and enslaved people, completed the flag in about seven weeks in 1813. Visit her former home to learn about the flag's place in history and the unusual life of this 19th century businesswoman.

Count the stars! This photo shows the flag flown in 1814. How many states were there then?

Federal Hill Park

Located just a short walk from the Inner Harbor, Federal Hill Park offers one of the best views in the city. Its location on a tall hill by the harbor made it an ideal watch tower and military outpost during the War of 1812 and the Civil War. Since 1880, Federal Hill has hosted a public park with a playground, basketball court, and historical monuments.

Little Italy

After a day of sightseeing, enjoy a delicious meal at one of the dozens of Italian restaurants and bakeries in Little Italy, a cozy neighborhood founded by Italian immigrants just a few blocks from the Inner Harbor.

Babe Ruth Birthplace and Museum

Baseball superstar George Herman "Babe" Ruth was born in Baltimore's Pigtown neighborhood in 1895. He grew up getting in trouble on the streets of Baltimore, and entered St. Mary's Industrial School for Boys in 1902, where he started playing baseball. He played for the Baltimore Orioles before gaining fame with the Boston Red Sox and the New York Yankees. The house where he was born is now a museum where you can learn more about Babe Ruth and his place in the game of baseball.

Phoenix Shot Tower

The Phoenix Shot Tower was built in 1828. At 215 feet tall, it was the tallest building in the United States for 18 years. But it wasn't there to let people see the view—this tower was a factory that produced ammunition for hunting rifles. Molten lead was poured through openings at the top of the tower. As the bits of lead fell, they spun and cooled into smooth "drops." In 1924, a group of citizens bought the tower and presented it to the City of Baltimore to be a museum.

Carroll Mansion

Learn about 200 years of history at the winter home of Charles Carroll, a signer of the Declaration of Independence. Before becoming a museum, the house served as a saloon, a furniture store, a school, and a recreation center.

Charles Carroll

Fells Point

Fells Point is a great place to get a taste of everything that makes Baltimore great, with historic cobblestone streets, classic Baltimore rowhouses, and many restaurants and shops. Walk along the waterfront, grab a bite to eat at the historic Broadway Market, and browse new music releases at The Sound Garden, one of the country's top independent music stores.

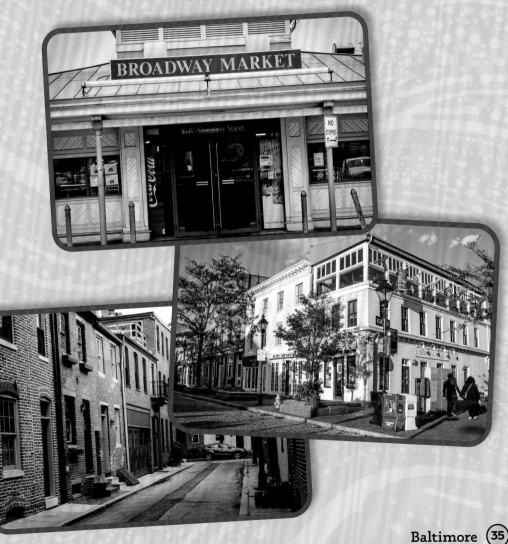

Things to See in Baltimore

Douglass Place: As an enslaved teenager in the 1830s, Frederick Douglass worked in the shipyards of Fells Point. In 1891, having become a renowned orator and abolitionist, he returned to the area and built five rowhouses on the site of an abandoned church, in order to provide affordable homes for the city's Black residents. You can visit these historic homes today.

W.E.B. DuBois House: One of the founders of the NAACP, W.E.B DuBois lived in Baltimore from 1939 to 1950. A scholar and author, DuBois was one of the most important figures in the Civil Rights Movement. His house was declared a Baltimore Landmark in 2008.

W.E.B DuBois

Edgar Allan Poe House: Visit the house that the celebrated poet and author lived in from 1833–1835 and learn about Poe's life and mysterious death in Baltimore.

Lexington Market: Founded in 1782, Lexington Market is the oldest market in America. In the mid-1800s, it was the most famous market in the world. Stop in and check out its more than 100 different stalls selling everything from Maryland crabcakes to fruits and vegetables, and taste a little bit of history.

Patterson Bowling Center: Duckpin bowling was invented in Baltimore in the late 1800s or early 1900s. This variation on traditional tenpin bowling uses smaller balls and pins. Duckpin bowling quickly gained popularity all along the East Coast. Try it for yourself at Patterson Bowling Center, built in 1927, the oldest duckpin bowling alley in the country.

Baltimore's Musical Heritage

Baltimore has a long and varied musical history; here are some of the people and places that made B-more sing!

Eubie Blake National Jazz Institute and Cultural Center: Pianist James Hubert "Eubie" Blake, born in Baltimore in 1883, was one of the most important figures in ragtime and jazz music. This center named for him brings together people from different backgrounds for performances and classes in dance, vocal and instrumental music, visual arts, and spoken word.

James Hubert "Eubie" Blake

Baltimore Symphony Orchestra: The Baltimore Symphony Orchestra (BSO) is one of the world's great musical groups. Established in 1916, the BSO brings dozens of concerts and workshops to audiences each year, including everything from classical music to calypso fusion. In 2007, the BSO made history when Maestra Marin Alsop became the first woman to lead a major American orchestra.

Chick Webb Recreation Center: William Henry "Chick" Webb was born in Baltimore in 1909. He taught himself to play drums. As a teenager, he went to Harlem and quickly rose through the jazz clubs and gained the nickname "The King of Swing." He vowed to fund a recreation center for Baltimore's Black families, who were barred from swimming in white pools due to segregation. After he died in 1939, others made his dream come true, opening the still-busy Chick Webb Memorial Recreation Center in 1947.

Billie Holiday Alley: Famed singer Billie Holiday grew up with relatives in Baltimore, in a childhood full of pain and trauma. In 1929, she went to Harlem, New York, where she would transform into the jazz legend called "Lady Day." Today, the block of Durham Street where she grew up is covered with murals and painted screens honoring Holiday.

Cab Calloway: "Hi-de-ho!" That was the famous call of Cab Calloway, wildly popular singer, actor, and bandleader in the 1930s and 1940s. Calloway grew up in Baltimore, honing his voice in the choir at Grace Presbyterian Church before moving to Chicago, where his performing career would take off.

Tupac Shakur: Before moving to California and becoming one of the most famous rappers of all time in the early 1990s, Tupac Shakur spent his teen years attending the Baltimore School for the Arts. He participated in rap battles at the Inner Harbor and even won a contest put on by the Enoch Pratt Free Library with a rap about getting a library card.

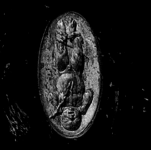

BILLIE HOLIDAY
⦿ -- 1915 - 1959 -- ⦿

"MOM AND POP WERE JUST A
COUPLE OF KIDS WHEN THEY
GOT MARRIED. HE WAS
EIGHTEEN SHE WAS SIXTEEN
AND I WAS THREE"

Seasons in the City

Like snowy days? We've got those! Like to stroll under the sun? We've got that, too. But Baltimore is protected from most extreme weather by the Chesapeake Bay and Atlantic Ocean in the east and the Appalachian Mountains in the west.

Winter: January is Baltimore's coldest month, with temperatures averaging between 31°F and 43°F. But cold winds may blow and snow may fall anytime between December and March. Though Baltimore only gets about 10-12 days of snow per year, heavy snowfalls sometimes shut down the city. If you see snowflakes in the forecast, make like a local and stock up on bread, milk, and toilet paper!

Spring: Snow and wind may continue into March. But by April, spring is in full swing in Baltimore! Enjoy sunshiny days and warmer daytime temperatures averaging between 54°F and 75°F. Even if the occasional rainy day forces you inside, you won't mind when you see the trees and gardens unfurling with spring colors. Maryland experiences an average of three tornadoes each year in the late spring and early summer, but they tend to be relatively mild and cause minor damage.

Summer: Summer in Baltimore is hot and humid. Humidity in July and August often reaches 75 percent. Daytime temperatures average 85°F to 89°F; even at night, the temperature rarely goes below 67°F. Pack your sunglasses and sunscreen! But pack your umbrella, too—about a third of summer days in Baltimore will have some rain. Though hurricanes rarely hit Baltimore, the city often experiences heavy rains, high winds, and even flash flooding from hurricanes moving up the East Coast in August and September.

Autumn: In autumn, the humidity finally lets up, but there are still plenty of sunny, clear days with daytime temperatures averaging 58°F to 80°F. As the weather slides into cooler, crisper days, many city residents take part in the longstanding tradition of "leaf peeping," or finding glorious views of changing leaves in local parks and streets.

GETTING AROUND

BALTIMORE

Most Baltimore residents get around by car or bus. But here are some other fun ways to get around Charm City!

Charm City Circulator: The easiest way to get around Baltimore's downtown is to hop on the Charm City Circulator, a fleet of free shuttle buses that run every 15–25 minutes.

Metro Subway Link: Baltimore's subway is small—only one 15.5-mile track that runs from Johns Hopkins Hospital to Owings Mills, a suburb of Baltimore. But it's a good way to get from downtown to other parts of the city like the Maryland Zoo.

By Water: Baltimore's Water Taxi connects waterfront neighborhoods around the Inner Harbor, including Fells Point, Federal Hill, and Fort McHenry. It runs from April to October. The free Harbor Connector boat is also available on weekdays to connect several major points.

Light RailLink: With 32 stops, this tram system runs on a north-south route that links points between the northern suburb of Hunt Valley and Baltimore/Washington International Thurgood Marshall Airport, south of the city. You'll find it easy to get to major spots like Oriole Park at Camden Yards and the Baltimore Convention Center with the Light RailLink. For destinations to the east and west, connect to one of the extensive network of city buses.

Museums— Go See 'Em!

Port Discovery Children's Museum: Port Discovery has tons of exhibits that ask kids of all ages to please touch, play, and have fun! Challenge yourself with the four-story SkyClimber and go down the giant Storm Slide. Learn about navigation on a life-sized cargo ship. Learn about art, science, math and more in fun exhibits that teach while you play.

Maryland Science Center: What started in 1797 as the Maryland Academy of Sciences, an amateur scientific society, is now a top science museum for kids and families. The Maryland Science Center serves up interactive exhibits and cool experiments in its spot overlooking the Inner Harbor. Explore the mysteries of dinosaurs, learn about physics in Newton's Alley, take a trip inside the human body to learn how your organs work, and learn about the cosmos as you catch a show in the Davis Planetarium.

National Great Blacks in Wax Museum: The National Great Blacks in Wax Museum was established in 1983 to teach about African American history through exhibits featuring life-sized wax figures. It was the first of its kind in the US. Over 100 wax figures and scenes explore topics like the history of the Atlantic Slave Trade (including a model ship), Blacks in the military, Black heroes, and great Black entrepreneurs.

Reginald F. Lewis Museum of Maryland African American History and Culture: The museum's collection represents over 400 years of history, telling the story of Maryland's African American community. Explore artifacts from the era of slavery, the history of jazz, political campaigns, and more.

More Museums!

B&O Railroad Museum: Explore historic trains, learn about railroading culture, and, of course, take a train ride or two! Built on the site where the Baltimore and Ohio Railroad, America's first commercial railroad, was founded in 1827, the B&O Railroad Museum has the oldest and largest collection of American trains and railroad artifacts in the world.

Baltimore Museum of Industry: Baltimore was once a seaport town full of factories, steel mills, and shipyards. The Baltimore Museum of Industry preserves that past with interactive exhibits for kids and families that tell the story of the machines and businesses that built our modern world. Step back in time to explore a 1910 pharmacy, learn how to set type in a 1930s print shop, and walk through an 1865 oyster cannery.

Baltimore Streetcar Museum: From 1859 to 1963, streetcars—first pulled by horses and later electric—carried passengers around the city. Tour these vintage vehicles and take a ride on one yourself at the Baltimore Streetcar Museum, home to dozens of streetcars dating back to 1859.

Dr. Samuel D. Harris National Museum of Dentistry: Sink your teeth into these interactive exhibits! Learn about the history of dental practices from ancient times to the present. (Did you know that in colonial times, people would go to a blacksmith to have a tooth pulled? Yikes!) The Dr. Samuel D. Harris National Museum of Dentistry houses more than 40,000 artifacts.

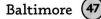

Outdoor Art in Baltimore

Sculpture Gardens at the Baltimore Museum of Art: Explore 33 modern and contemporary sculptures spread over three acres, from the 14-foot-tall bright-red shapes of Alexander Calder's *The 100-Yard Dash* (1969) to the whimsical bronze *Large Boxing Hare on Anvil* by Barry Flanagan (1984).

Graffiti Alley: This is the only place in the state of Maryland where graffiti is both legal and encouraged! In this L-shaped alley, you'll be surrounded by an ever-changing gallery of work—on the walls and the ground alike—from hundreds of different artists. Graffiti Alley is a safe space for graffiti artists to take their time as they work, so that they can try new techniques and connect with other artists.

Equilibrium Mural by Amy Sherald: This giant mural, which graces the wall of the historic Parkway Theatre at the center of the city, pays tribute to the strength of African American women with its image of a woman balancing a pole across her shoulders, while a heart dangles on a chain from one hand. Baltimore artist Amy Sherald is best known for her portrait of former First Lady Michelle Obama.

Pool No. 2: From the time it was built in 1921 until Baltimore's pools were finally desegregated in 1956, Pool No. 2 in Druid Hill Park was where thousands of Black residents swam. After desegregation, Pool No. 2 closed. In 1999, African American artist Joyce J. Scott turned it into a piece of thoughtful outdoor art. The pool is now filled in with dirt and grass, but the original ladders, lifeguard chair, and diving board stand nearby. Red and orange patterns in the concrete are based on African symbols of peace.

Baltimore LED Art Billboard: On a 52-foot-tall electronic billboard at the entrance to the Baltimore Art District, images of drawings, sculptures, paintings, and other artworks alternate with the usual advertisements. The artists featured range from amateurs to professionals and their portfolios can be found on the billboard's website. It's a free digital gallery anyone can view right on the street!

Art Museums

Baltimore Museum of Art: Where can you visit 95,000 works of art for free? The Baltimore Museum of Art! Here you'll find paintings, drawings, sculptures, and more from all over the world, representing ancient to modern times. The museum also houses the world's largest collection of works by artist Henri Matisse.

Bromo Seltzer Arts Tower: One of the most recognizable buildings in Baltimore, this tower was built to be the headquarters of the Emerson Drug Company in 1911. It was modeled on the Palazzo Vecchio in Florence, Italy. Originally, the 306-foot tall clock tower was topped by a giant blue bottle of Bromo Seltzer, the company's most famous product. Now the tower is a gallery and workspace for Baltimore artists, and hosts free exhibitions and performances. It's also home to the Emerson/Maryland Glass Museum.

Walters Art Museum: It's also free to visit the Walters Art Museum, which is housed in five historic buildings. The Walters is an international leader in protecting manuscripts and art, and its collection shows it: the 36,000 objects on display include everything from Ethiopian manuscripts to books from Southeast Asia to ancient Roman sarcophagi.

American Visionary Art Museum: Perhaps no other museum captures the quirky spirit of Baltimore better than the American Visionary Art Museum, which is dedicated to showcasing work by self-taught artists expressing an "innate personal vision." The AVAM's three buildings are stuffed with work that will make you smile, laugh, or drop your jaw. Be sure to press the button on the mirror-spangled Magic Farting Post by Bob Bowman—and hear the sounds of a professional farting competition. (Yes, that's a real thing!)

Charm City Creatives

Artscape

Don't miss America's largest free arts festival, featuring hundreds of arts exhibits, activities, concerts, and family events—plus lots of yummy food! Artscape began in 1982 as a way to bring Baltimore's different communities together through the arts.

Crowds pack Artscape events.

Maryland Film Festival

The event takes place each spring at Baltimore's historic Parkway Theater, and its mission is to bring film to everyone. The multi-day festival showcases feature films and shorts alongside filmmaking programs and panels, with special schedules for family-friendly films and films with a Baltimore connection.

Crazy for Comic Books

Baltimore-based Diamond Comic Distributors is the largest distributor of English-language comic books in the world. It offers over 2,500 new products per month. That's a lot of comics! Diamond originated Free Comic Book Day, where shops worldwide give away comic books. Also keeping comic book fever alive: Baltimore Comic-Con, a three-day event each autumn where thousands of fans celebrate everything comics-related with panels, celebrity appearances, costume contests, and more.

National Stars from B-More

Many well-known creators and performers were born or raised in Baltimore, including actors Edward Norton, Josh Charles, Julie Bowen, David Hasselhoff, Parker Posey, puppeteer Kevin Clash (best known as the voice of Elmo), and musicians Frank Zappa, Sisqó, Tori Amos, and Philip Glass. Bands that got their start in Baltimore include Dru Hill, Beach House, Wye Oak, and OXES.

How to SPEAK Baltimore

Every town has words and phrases that only make sense to the people who live there. But Baltimore also has its own unique way of speaking known as the "Baltimore accent." Here's a glossary (in Baltimore-ese) of some common Baltimore words and phrases to get you started:

BALMER OR BALDAMOR
the city's name.

curry
to carry.

hon
a term of endearment used with friends and strangers alike, short for "honey."

lor
little.

downy ocean
Ocean City, Maryland, where Baltimoreans hit the beach in the summer. Example: "You going downy ocean, hon?"

warsh
to wash.

WOODER
what you warsh with: water.

zink
where you warsh with the wooder— in the sink.

Merlin
Maryland.

How 'bout dem O's?
A way to start a conversation about Baltimore's beloved baseball team, the Orioles.

Hon Culture

What is a Hon?

The figure of the "hon"—a woman with a tall beehive hairdo and bright clothes and jewelry—has become one of the major symbols of Baltimore's quirky personality. The hon is a tribute to the working-class women of Baltimore's past. They dressed and did their hair to stand out in jobs where women were supposed to fade into the background. Whether they were waitressing, housekeeping, or taking in laundry, they called their customers "hon" rather than "sir" or "ma'am." And the name stuck.

Hons on Stage and Screen

Baltimore filmmaker John Waters has brought the Baltimore hon to international audiences. His most famous film, *Hairspray* (1988), is set in 1960s Baltimore. It tells the story of 16-year-old Tracy Turnblad, a girl with big hair and big dreams of getting onto a popular TV dance show. The story has themes of body image, racial justice, and identity. Hairspray was turned into a Tony-Award-winning stage musical that opened on Broadway in 2002. Then a movie was made of the stage musical in 2007.

HONfest

For two days each summer, the Baltimore neighborhood of Hampden, known for its quirky shops and restaurants, is home to HONFest. Thousands of people show up dressed in beehive wigs, colorful clothes, and costume jewelry. They celebrate the hon with music, dancing, booths, and food. And of course, there's a contest to find Baltimore's Best Hon!

How to Spot a Baltimore Hon

Beehive hairdo (with lots and lots of hairspray!). The hon's motto is "the higher the hair the closer to heaven!"

Blue eyeshadow

Glasses (often cat-eye or with rhinestones)

Bows, feathers, or flowers

Bold jewelry

Leopard print

BALTIMORE: It's Weird!

Mr. Trash Wheel

What's that giant googly-eyed creature gobbling plastic bottles, cigarette butts, mattresses, and tires out of the water before they can flow into the Inner Harbor? It's Mr. Trash Wheel! The first machine of its kind in the world, Mr. Trash Wheel appeared in 2014. Using solar power, plus power generated by a water wheel, it rakes up to 38,000 pounds of trash per day onto his conveyer belt. He's become a hit on social media, and even has his own website.

East Coast National Championship Kinetic Sculpture Race

The American Visionary Art Museum hosts this odd race each year. You'll see teams pedaling works of art, each made from trash and spare parts. Teams can only use human power to propel their sculptures over the 15-mile course. They race on water, mud, sand, and roads. Winners get medals, but they also award "The Next to Last Award" and "The Golden Dinosaur Award" for the most exciting breakdown of the race.

The Goucher Mummy

One of the most unusual sights you'll see in Baltimore: the mummified remains of an adult woman from the Ptolemaic Period of ancient Egypt (305–330 BCE). Dr. John Goucher originally brought the mummified woman to Baltimore in 1895. In the 1980s, the Johns Hopkins Archeological Museum began using radiography and other computer technology to learn more about the mummified woman and how she lived. The museum's current exhibit helps visitors to understand the woman as a real person, not just a curiosity.

Papermoon Diner

At this diner, you'll chow down on favorite comfort foods like pancakes, sandwiches, and milkshakes. But you'll be surrounded by an ever-changing display of what restaurant owner Un Kim calls "living art." No plain booths or walls here; every surface is covered with the stuff of pop culture—Pez dispensers, old lunchboxes, carousel horses, and lots of mannequins. It's bizarre and a little creepy—and very Baltimore.

Famous People Today

John Waters

No one represents the offbeat spirit of Baltimore better than this award-winning filmmaker, writer, and photographer. Waters has lived and worked in the city his whole life. His cult classics include *Hairspray* (1988) and *Cry-Baby* (1990). He's also the author of 10 books. His photographs have been shown in galleries worldwide. An icon of the queer community and of outsiders everywhere, Waters challenges people's expectations through his work.

After graduating from the Baltimore School for the Arts, actor Jada Pinkett Smith got her big break in 1991 on the TV series *A Different World*. She went on to star in many films, including *Menace II Society* (1993), *The Nutty Professor* (1996), *Scream 2* (1997), and three *Matrix* films. She has been candid about her diagnosis with alopecia, an autoimmune disorder that causes hair loss. She's tackled this and other tough topics on her talk show, *Red Table Talk*.

Jada Pinkett Smith

Ta-Nehisi Coates is an award-winning journalist and author of nonfiction and novels. In 2015, he won the National Book Award for *Between the World and Me*. His work explores what it means to be Black in America. He has also written *Black Panther* and *Captain America* comics. He is known for a style that brings the rhythms of hip-hop to the page.

Ta-Nehisi Coates

Michael Phelps

With a record-setting 28 Olympic medals—23 of them gold—swimmer Michael Phelps has been called the greatest Olympic athlete of all time. As a child, he struggled because of attention deficit hyperactivity disorder (ADHD). Swimming helped him focus his energy. By age 10, he was setting national records; by age 15, he was winning medals in his first of five Olympic Games. Through the Michael Phelps Foundation, he brings swimming and water safety instruction to people around the world.

What People Do in
BALTIMORE

About 2.8 million people live in the Baltimore metro area. Here are the most common ways they make a living.

Government

More than 11,000 employees work at the Social Security Administration headquarters complex just outside of Baltimore. They run insurance programs that benefit about 64 million people including retirees, children, and people with disabilities. Right down the street is the headquarters of the Centers for Medicare and Medicaid Services, which provide health insurance to more than 100 million people.

medicine

Baltimore is a center for medical advances. Johns Hopkins Hospital is often ranked as one of the top hospitals in the country. Shock Trauma at the University of Maryland Medical Center is the nation's first hospital dedicated to treating critically injured patients. More than 100,000 people work in the healthcare industry in and around Baltimore.

Higher Education

With 76 colleges and universities calling the Baltimore area home, higher education is a major field. Johns Hopkins University alone has more than 26,000 employees.

manufacturing and Retail

Several global companies have their headquarters in Baltimore, including Under Armour athletic wear, Royal Farms convenience stores, and McCormick and Company, makers of flavorings and spices including Baltimore's beloved Old Bay.

SALE

Giving Back and Doing Good

Important national charities as well as local nonprofit agencies make Baltimore a place that is filled with people helping people.

Bea Gaddy Family Centers

Dr. Bea Gaddy (1933-2001) grew up in poverty. She dedicated her life to taking care of Baltimore's poor and homeless population. She founded the Patterson Park Emergency Food Center, ran youth programs, established free Thanksgiving dinners, and served on the Baltimore City Council. Today, the Bea Gaddy Family Centers carry on her legacy of providing food and assistance to the city's most vulnerable people.

Annie E. Casey Foundation

Founded in 1948, this group has been headquartered in Baltimore since 1994. It gives money to support children, families, and communities facing poverty and limited opportunities.

THE ANNIE E. CASEY FOUNDATION

National Federation of the Blind

Headquartered in Baltimore, the National Federation of the Blind is the nation's oldest and largest organization of blind people. Since its founding in 1940, the organization has defended the rights of blind Americans and established programs to support visually impaired people.

NATIONAL FEDERATION
OF THE BLIND
LOUISIANA
Live the life you want.

In 2018, the Baltimore Orioles wore jerseys with Braille symbols in honor of the hometown NFB.

The Associated: Jewish Federation of Baltimore

Known around town simply as "The Associated," this nonprofit organization began over 100 years ago. Its mission today is to protect and support Jewish people worldwide through Jewish values including charity and social justice. The Associated's programs include jobs help, education, and summer camps.

The **Associated**
Jewish Federation of Baltimore

Catholic Relief Services

From its headquarters in Baltimore, Catholic Relief Services provides support to people in 100 countries around the world, responding to natural disasters, disease, and poverty. The organization was founded in 1943 to help refugees of World War II.

CRS
CATHOLIC RELIEF SERVICES

Eat the Baltimore Way

Baltimore food is about more than crabs (see next page). Dig in!

Snowballs: During hot and sticky Baltimore summers, snowball stands pop up everywhere. Unlike snow cones or Hawaiian ice, the Baltimore snowball uses finely shaved ice covered in flavored syrup. Try a classic flavor like sweet egg custard or skylite, which will turn your tongue blue! To eat your snowball like a true Baltimorean, add marshmallow topping. City residents have been enjoying Baltimore snowballs since the early 1800s.

Lemon Peppermint Sticks: Cut a lemon in half, insert a thick peppermint stick, and there you go: a yummy sweet and sour treat for a Baltimore summer day. The peppermint stick acts as a straw to suck up the lemon juice, and you can eat it when you're done! No one quite knows who invented these quintessentially Baltimore sweets, but you'll see them at every summer fair and festival in Charm City.

Berger Cookies: These unique cookies are the perfect gift to take home from your trip to Baltimore. A Berger cookie is a soft, cake-like cookie, hand-dipped in thick, sweet fudgey icing. These cookies have been around since 1835, when German immigrant Henry Berger came to Maryland and opened a bakery.

Scrapple: It may sound gross: a breakfast meat made from pig scraps (liver, kidneys, skin, spleen, and more) ground up and mixed with cornmeal, buckwheat flour, onions, seasonings, and maple syrup. But Baltimoreans will tell you it's crispy, delicious, and a perfect side dish for eggs. You can enjoy scrapple with ketchup or syrup or on its own.

Black Bottom Cupcakes: Can't decide between a chocolate cupcake and cheesecake? The classic Baltimore black bottom cupcake gives you the best of both worlds! With chocolate cake on the outside and a gooey cream cheese center, these sweets have been a staple of city bakeries for decades.

All About Crabs!!

Marylanders love crabs so much that the blue crab has become a symbol of Baltimore and its state. Maryland blue crabs are delicious in many dishes such as crab cakes and crab soup.

Messy, Messy

To enjoy them like a Baltimorean, plunk yourself down at a table covered in brown paper. Prepare to get messy while you pick the sweet buttery meat out of a pile of steamed crabs and use a mallet to smash open those claws.

No Candles Here

Crab cakes are another popular way to enjoy this seafood. Crab meat is mixed with bread crumbs, mayonnaise, and spices. The mix is made into burger-like disks and fried. Yum!

Why Baltimore?

Fishermen have been harvesting blue crabs from the Chesapeake Bay for hundreds of years. Maryland's blue crabs are known as the best in the country for their flavor and taste. The reason is Maryland's climate: as the crabs hibernate over the winter, they build up fat reserves that deepen their flavor. About half of the blue crabs harvested in the country come from Maryland.

Old Bay Seasoning

Every Marylander knows that those steamed crabs had better be seasoned with Old Bay! German immigrant Gustav Brunn invented this kicky blend of 18 different spices in the 1940s. It was designed to be the perfect crab seasoning. But you can also sprinkle Old Bay on foods from chicken to deviled eggs to popcorn. In 1990, Baltimore spice manufacturer McCormick and Company bought the secret recipe and took over production of the beloved classic.

Oriole Park at Camden Yards

In 1992, the new home of the Baltimore Orioles opened—and 3.57 million people bought tickets in the first year alone. The stadium itself became a superstar and would influence the architecture of baseball stadiums around the country. Unlike boring multipurpose suburban stadiums, Oriole Park at Camden Yards was situated right in the heart of downtown, just steps from the Inner Harbor. It was a return to old-fashioned, baseball-only ballparks that reflected the city's unique character and history. In the years since its opening, most new stadiums have been built in city centers.

The stadium features a hand-laid red brick exterior with arches that provide a historic feel.

The foul poles came from the Orioles' previous home at Memorial Stadium.

It's built up against the eight-story B&O Railroad Warehouse, which dates to 1899.

Cast-iron gates reflect the city's steelmaking past.

Go, Baltimore Sports!

Baltimore has devoted fans of all sorts of sports. Find out who they root for here!

BALTIMORE ORIOLES

Joined Major League Baseball in 1901. One year later, the team moved to St. Louis and became the St. Louis Browns. In 1954, the Browns moved back to Baltimore and took on the city's traditional baseball team name, the Orioles.

Cool Stuff:

➤ The Orioles won the World Series in 1966, 1970, and 1983.

➤ In 1995, shortstop Cal Ripken, Jr. set a new Major League Baseball record for most consecutive games played—2,131 games. He finished with 2,632 consecutive games played between 1982 and 1998.

Big Names: Brooks Robinson, Boog Powell, Jim Palmer, Frank Robinson, Eddie Murray, Cal Ripken, Jr., Mike Mussina

Home: Oriole Park at Camden Yards

Cal Ripken, Jr.

FAST FACT
The Baltimore oriole is Maryland's state bird. The male oriole's black and golden orange colors are similar to the colors of the Maryland flag.

BALTIMORE RAVENS

Joined the National Football League in 1950. The team played as the Cleveland Browns until 1996, when it moved to Baltimore and was renamed the Ravens.

Cool Stuff:

➤ The Ravens have won two Super Bowls, in 2001 and 2013.

➤ The team got its name from Edgar Allan Poe's famous poem, "The Raven."

Big Names: Ray Lewis, Lamar Jackson, Ed Reed, Johnathan Ogden, Terrell Suggs, Jamal Lewis, Joe Flacco, Haloti Ngata

Home: M & T Bank Stadium

FAST FACT

Baltimore used to have a different NFL team, the Colts, from 1950 to 1984. In March 1984, the team's owner moved the Colts to Indianapolis under cover of night, shocking Baltimore fans.

BALTIMORE BLAST

Joined Major Arena Soccer League in 2014. The team was originally the Houston Summit. It came to Baltimore in 1980 as a member of the Major Indoor Soccer League.

Cool Stuff:

➤ The team has won 10 championships since 1980. The Baltimore Blast is heavily involved in the community, running camps and other programs.

➤ Arena soccer is played six-on-six on a hockey-rink-sized field.

Big Names: Stan Stamenkovic, Mike Stankovic, Pat Ercoli, Heinz Wirtz, Nick Mangione, Scott Manning

Home: SECU Arena at Towson University

The Preakness Stakes

Each year on the third Saturday in May, thoroughbred racing fans descend on Baltimore's Pimlico Race Course for the Preakness Stakes. This 1 and 3/16-mile race is the second race of America's Triple Crown (which also includes the Kentucky Derby and the Belmont Stakes). The Preakness was first run at Pimlico in 1873.

Lacrosse

Lacrosse is wildly popular throughout Maryland. In this fast-paced team sport, players use a long-handled stick with a net on the end to scoop, throw, and catch a small ball. They try to get the ball into the opposing team's goal while protecting their own. It's the oldest team sport in North America, and was played by Indigenous people in the US and Canada long before it was first written about by a Jesuit missionary in 1636.

Many Maryland middle schools, high schools, colleges, and universities have their own championship-winning lacrosse teams. Club teams for kids and adults play throughout the state, so everyone can join in the fun. US Lacrosse Headquarters is located just outside Baltimore.

FAST FACT
Lacrosse is the official team sport of Maryland. What's the official state sport? Jousting!

COLLEGE TOWN

Baltimore is home to some of the top colleges and universities in the country. Here are a few:

JOHNS HOPKINS UNIVERSITY

Founded: 1876
Students: 28,890
Popular Majors: engineering, biological and biomedical sciences, social sciences, health professions, computer and information sciences
Fast Fact: Johns Hopkins was the country's first research university.

George Peabody Library at Johns Hopkins.

MORGAN STATE UNIVERSITY

Founded: 1867
Students: 7,634
Popular Majors: business, management, marketing, engineering
Fast Fact: The campus of this Historically Black College/University (HBCU) was named as a National Treasure by the National Trust for Historic Preservation.

UNIVERSITY OF MARYLAND, COLLEGE PARK

Founded: 1856
Students: 41,272
Popular Majors: social sciences, computer and information sciences, business, management, marketing, engineering, biological and biomedical sciences
Fast Facts: The campus has its own golf course and its own farm.

MARYLAND INSTITUTE COLLEGE OF ART (MICA)

Founded: 1826
Students: 1,892
Popular Majors: illustration, architecture, film and video, game design, art history, graphic design, painting
Fast Fact: MICA has been granting degrees longer than any other college of art and design in the US.

LOYOLA UNIVERSITY MARYLAND

Founded: 1852
Students: 5,140
Popular Majors: business, management, marketing, communication, journalism
Fast Fact: The school was established by Jesuit priests and named for the founder of their order, St. Ignatius of Loyola.

It's Alive! Animals in Baltimore

Even though Baltimore is a bustling city, many animals call it home. Here are some of the creatures you can find in the city's parks, green spaces, alleys, and waterways.

Gray squirrels

White-tailed deer

Red foxes

Northern cardinals

Rats!

Like many big cities, Baltimore has lots of rats. Some Baltimoreans have embraced the rat as a symbol of the city. Like Baltimore's people, rats are underdogs and survivors. Don't be surprised if you see Baltimore rat stickers proudly displayed!

Ospreys

These birds of prey use the[ir] claws to catch fish. Osprey[s were] wiped out by pesticides in t[he] Chesapeake Bay is home to [ ] nesting pairs of ospreys ea[ch]

In the Chesapeake Bay

The nearby waters of the huge bay are filled with marine life of all kinds.

Pumpkinseed sunfish

Blue crabs

American eels

WE SAW IT AT THE ZOO

The Maryland Zoo began in the 1860s, when the superintendent of Druid Hill Park began caring for animals donated by city residents. The zoo was formally established by the state legislature in 1876. Its collection includes 130 species. The zoo is divided into four main areas (below). But don't miss the Main Valley Exhibit, where you can see the zoo's original Victorian-era cages and learn how zoo habitats have changed over the years.

Penguin Coast: Learn about African penguins and other seabirds. The Maryland Zoo runs the largest African penguin breeding colony in North America.

Northern Passage: Visit with grizzly bears, a bald eagle, and other animals of the northern hemisphere.

African Journey: Feed a giraffe, visit a lion, and wave to an elephant as you explore the wildlife of Africa.

Maryland Wilderness: Learn about bog, marsh, mountain stream, cave, woods, and meadow habitats as you explore the native species of Maryland. Don't miss the Farmyard, where you'll get to groom a goat, pet an alpaca, and slide down the Barn silo slide.

Druid Hill Park

Druid Hill Park, which houses the Maryland Zoo, was one of the first great urban parks in the US. The city bought the land from the Druid Hill Estate in 1860. Its designers used the natural flow of the landscape to create carriage, walking, and horseback riding paths, plus picnic groves and a lake. Check out the country's second-oldest Victorian glass conservatory, the Howard P. Rawlings Conservatory and Botanic Gardens.

Spooky Sites

Are ghosts and spirits real? No one knows for sure. But here are some places in Baltimore that are pretty spooky either way!

Westminster Burying Ground opened in 1786. It's known as one of America's most haunted cemeteries. Soldiers from the American Revolution and the War of 1812 are buried there. Some people claim to have seen the ghost of Lucia Watson, a teenager who died in 1816. Others say they saw the ghost of an old woman, wandering up and down the paths looking for her corpse, which was stolen by graverobbers.

The Poe Toaster: The most famous person buried in Westminster Burying Ground is author Edgar Allan Poe. From around 1949 until 2009, a mysterious person, face covered, would appear in the dark of night at Poe's grave every year on January 19, Poe's birthday. The figure would toast Poe and leave three red roses and a bottle on his grave. Though the tradition was much written about, the identity of the Poe Toaster was never uncovered.

ORIGINAL BURIAL PLACE OF
EDGAR ALLAN POE
FROM
OCTOBER 9, 1849,
UNTIL
NOVEMBER 17, 1875.

MRS. MARIA CLEMM, HIS MOTHER-IN-LAW
LIES UPON HIS RIGHT AND VIRGINIA
HIS WIFE, UPON HIS LEFT, UNDER
MONUMENT ERECTED TO HIM IN THIS
CEMETERY.

The Horse You Came in On Saloon: Another spooky site connected to Poe is The Horse You Came in On Saloon—it was the last place he went before his death in 1849. Built on the cobblestone streets of Fells Point, it dates back to 1775. It's the country's oldest continually operated saloon.

Poe is said to haunt the building, emptying glasses left out for him and even pulling barstools out from under customers! Staff members claim that other unnamed spirits open and close doors, shatter glasses, open the cash register, and turn lights on and off.

Elijah Bond's Ouija Board Grave: Seances were all the rage in the late 1800s. In 1890, Elijah Bond and his friends gathered at a Baltimore hotel. There, they developed the Ouija Board, a mass-produced board game for contacting the spirits. Bond is buried in Green Mount Cemetery. His grave is easy to find—it's the one with a headstone carved like a giant Ouija Board!

Curtis Creek Ship Graveyard: South of the city, the Patapsco River flows into Curtis Creek. There, you can see the Curtis Creek Ship Graveyard, the abandoned hulks of dozens of ships, ranging from early 20th century wooden freighters to ferries and barges. When the ships were no longer useful and couldn't be turned into scrap, they were brought here and intentionally sunk. One member of this ghostly fleet is the three-masted schooner *William T. Parker*. Abandoned in North Carolina in 1899, it drifted up and down the Atlantic coast before being captured and sunk in Curtis Creek.

BALTIMORE FIRSTS

First umbrella factory in the US: William Beehler founded it in Baltimore in 1828. His company's motto: "Born in Baltimore, raised everywhere."

First publicly supported symphony orchestra in the world: The Baltimore Symphony Orchestra began in 1916 as a branch of Baltimore's city government. In 1942, it became a private institution.

First shopping center in the US: Roland Park Shopping Center, built in 1895. This long, gabled building had another innovation—it was set back from the street to provide a parking lot. Roland Park Shopping Center still houses neighborhood shops and restaurants.

First railroad station in the US: Mount Clare Station opened in 1830 to serve the Baltimore and Ohio Railroad. The station is now part of the B&O Railroad Museum.

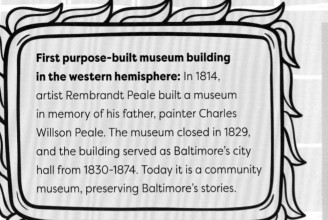

First purpose-built museum building in the western hemisphere: In 1814, artist Rembrandt Peale built a museum in memory of his father, painter Charles Willson Peale. The museum closed in 1829, and the building served as Baltimore's city hall from 1830-1874. Today it is a community museum, preserving Baltimore's stories.

First natural gas lights in the US: In 1816, at the Peale Museum. In 1817, the nation's first gas streetlamp was lit nearby. You can see a replica of it at the corner of North Holliday Street and East Baltimore Street.

First dental school in the world: The Baltimore College of Dental Surgery, which opened in 1840.

First electric streetcar in the US: The North Avenue-to-Hampden line switched from horse-drawn to electric streetcars on August 15, 1885. It cost just a nickel to ride!

First Southern US city to desegregate a public school: In 1952, local Civil Rights activists convinced the school board to admit African American students to Baltimore Polytechnic Institute, a high school. This was two years before the US Supreme Court's ruling in *Brown vs. Board of Education* made segregation illegal nationwide.

Not Far Away

There's more to explore! While you're visiting Baltimore, check out these day trips to places nearby.

All hands on deck! It's a beautiful day for sailing on the Chesapeake Bay!

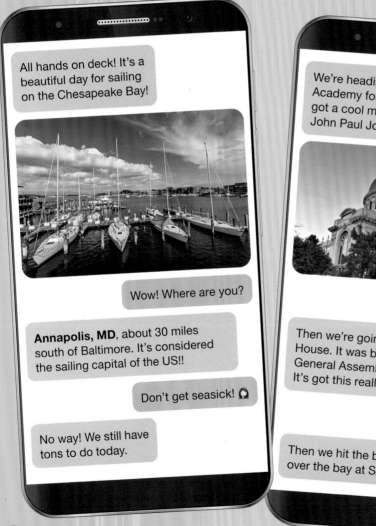

Wow! Where are you?

Annapolis, MD, about 30 miles south of Baltimore. It's considered the sailing capital of the US!!

Don't get seasick! 🎧

No way! We still have tons to do today.

We're heading over to the U.S. Naval Academy for a tour after this. It's got a cool museum, and the crypt of John Paul Jones is under the chapel!

Very cool!

Then we're going to the MD State House. It was built in 1779 and the MD General Assembly still uses it today. It's got this really cool wooden dome.

Then you get to rest?

Then we hit the beach! Gotta see sunset over the bay at Sandy Point State Park.

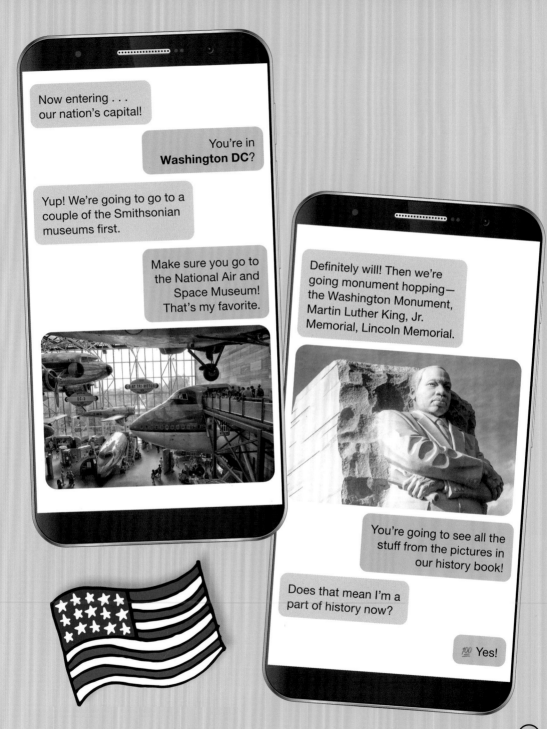

Now entering . . . our nation's capital!

You're in **Washington DC**?

Yup! We're going to go to a couple of the Smithsonian museums first.

Make sure you go to the National Air and Space Museum! That's my favorite.

Definitely will! Then we're going monument hopping— the Washington Monument, Martin Luther King, Jr. Memorial, Lincoln Memorial.

You're going to see all the stuff from the pictures in our history book!

Does that mean I'm a part of history now?

💯 Yes!

Off to catch the ferry!

Oooh! Where are you heading?

Smith Island. It's actually not just one island, but a collection of them in the marshes. No bridges = you can only get there by boat!

So . . . you're just going to sit around in the marshes?

No, silly! Smith Island has lots of shops and a great museum. Then we're going to check out the kayaking trail around the island. Might even do some proggin.

???

SMITH ISLAND

MARYLAND'S ONLY REMAINING INHABITED OFFSHORE ISLAND GROUP, NAMED FOR EARLY LAND OWNER HENRY SMITH. CHARTED BY CAPTAIN JOHN SMITH IN 1608 AS "THE RUSSELL ISLES." ENGLISH FARMERS JOHN EVANS AND JOHN TYLER CAME VIA ACCOMACK COUNTY VIRGINIA TO BECOME THE FIRST PERMANENT SETTLERS IN 1686. DURING THE REVOLUTIONARY WAR THE BRITISH USED THE ISLAND AS A BASE OF OPERATIONS. ONCE THE HOME OF JOSHUA THOMAS, FAMED METHODIST EVANGELIST WHO HELD THE FIRST CAMP MEETING ON THE ISLAND.

MARYLAND HISTORICAL TRUST
MARYLAND STATE HIGHWAY ADMINISTRATION

That's Smith Island talk for looking for arrowheads and other cool stuff in the marshes. The islanders have their own unique dialect.

Well, happy proggin then!

But the best part about this place is Smith Island Cake—layers and layers of chocolate-filled yumminess.

Oh! Bring me some!

Next stop, Frederick County, MD! So much Civil War history around here. The National Museum of Civil War Medicine, Monocacy National Battlefield, South Mountain State Battlefield Park . . .

Wow! That's a lot of history!

And that's not all. My favorite spot is **Catoctin Furnace**. It's a restored iron furnace village from the 1850s. You can walk around inside the furnace and everything! Plus there are tons of hiking trails and a waterfall too – Cunningham Falls.

Sign me up! Let's go camping there sometime.

Sister Cities Around the World

Can a city have a sister? It sure can—and Baltimore has nine of them! In 1956, the US government created the Sister Cities program to promote peace by connecting cities around the world.

Rotterdam, the Netherlands

Odesa, Ukraine

Changwon, South Korea

Piraeus, Greece

Alexandria, Egypt

Luxor, Egypt

Xiamen, China

Kawasaki, Japan

Gbarnga, Liberia

Baltimore's Sister Cities

Sister Cities in Action

Here are some examples of how the people of Baltimore are working with and helping their Sister Cities:

Alexandria, Egypt, and Luxor, Egypt: Baltimore and Luxor have been sister cities since 1978. In 1995, Baltimore paired with Alexandria as well. Over the years, the three cities have hosted exchange programs to promote education, technology, and business development, as well as education conferences and a project to improve water quality. Cultural programs in Baltimore have showcased the art, music, and history of Egypt.

Odesa, Ukraine: Since the Russian invasion of Ukraine in early 2022, the Baltimore-Odesa Sister Cities Committee has been busy providing first aid kits, refugee housing, and cybersecurity to Odesa's people. In Baltimore, there are plays and concerts to share Ukrainian culture with the people.

Changwon, South Korea: This is one of Baltimore's newest sister cities, with the agreement signed in 2019. Both port cities, they are working together to create cultural, educational, and professional exchanges to help their people get to know one another better. The cities also host programs and storytimes to share their history and culture.

Books

Balkan, Evan. *Secret Baltimore: A Guide to the Weird, Wonderful, and Obscure.* St. Louis, Reedy Press, 2020.

Friddell, Claudia. *Goliath: Hero of the Great Baltimore Fire.* Ann Arbor, MI: Sleeping Bear Press, 2010.

Gigliotti, Jim. *Who Was Edgar Allan Poe? Penguin Workshop, 2015.*

Kramer, Barbara. *Harriet Tubman.* Washington, D.C.: National Geographic Kids, 2019.

Langley, Sharon. *A Ride to Remember.* New York: Abrams, 2019.

Myers, Walter Dean. *Frederick Douglass.* New York: HarperCollins, 2017.

About the Author

Kathy MacMillan was born in Baltimore and has lived in and around the city her whole life. She is a writer, American Sign Language interpreter, librarian, and signing storyteller. She writes picture books, children's nonfiction, middle grade fantasy, and young adult fantasy. Find her online at KathyMacMillan.com or on Twitter and Instagram at @kathys_quill.

Web Sites

Visit Baltimore
   https://baltimore.org/

Baltimore National Heritage Area
   https://www.explorebaltimore.org/city-history

Chesapeake Bay Program
   https://www.chesapeakebay.net/

Digital Maryland
   https://www.digitalmaryland.org/

Maryland Women's Hall of Fame
   https://msa.maryland.gov/msa/educ/exhibits/
   womenshallfame/html/index.html

National Aquarium
   https://aqua.org/

Photo Credits and Thanks

Photos from Dreamstime, Library of Congress, Shutterstock, or Wikimedia unless otherwise noted. Alamy Stock Photo: The Picture Art Collection 15B; Niday Picture Library 15 bkgd; Edwin Remsberg 26B. AP Photos: Amy Davis/Baltimore Sun 59TR; Patrick Semansky 66C; Newscom: Scott Wachter/Icon SMI 72R; Bill Greenblatt/UPI 74T.

Artwork: Lemonade Pixel; Maps (6-7) by Jessica Nevins. Cover typography by Swell Type.

Thanks to our pals Nancy Ellwood, Jessica Rothenberg, and the fine folks at Arcadia Children's Books!

INDEX

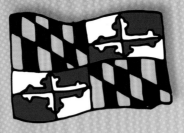

African Methodist Episcopal Church 28

American Visionary Art Museum 51, 58

Annapolis 86

Annie E. Casey Foundation 64

Antietam 18

Applachian Mountains 6

Arabbers 27

Artscape 52

Associated: Jewish Federation of Baltimore 65

Babe Ruth Birthplace and Museum 33

Baltimore Blast 74

Baltimore Clippers 16

Baltimore Colts 73

Baltimore & Ohio Railroad 16, 46, 71, 72

Baltimore & Ohio Railroad Museum 46

Baltimore Orioles 5, 21, 33, 55, 70-71

Baltimore Museum of Art 50

Baltimore Museum of Industry 46

Baltimore Ravens 73

Baltimore Streetcar Museum 47

Baltimore Symphony Orchestra 39, 84

Basilica of the National Shrine of the Assumption of the Blessed Virgin Mary 29

Bea Gaddy Family Centers, 64

Blake, Eubie 38

Bond, Elijah 83

Broadway Market 35Calvert, Cecil 9

Bromo Seltzer Arts Tower 50

Calder, Alexander 48

Calloway, Cab 39

Catholic Relief Services 64

Catoctin Furnace 89

Calvert, Sir George 8, 9

Carroll, Charles 34

Carroll Mansion 34

Channing, Rev. Dr. William Ellery 29

Charm City Circulator 42

Chesapeake Bay, the 6, 12, 69, 79, 86

Chessie 11

Chick Webb Recreation Center 38

Civil War 4, 9, 17, 18

Coates, Ta-Nehisi 61

Comic-Con 53

Continental Congress 15

crabs 68-69

Curtis Creek Ship Graveyard 83

Diamond Comic Distribution 53

Douglass, Frederick 24

Douglass Place 36

Druid Hill Park 81

East Coast National Championship Kinetic Sculpture Race 58

Eck, Johnny 25

Edgar Allan Poe House 37

Eubie Blake National Jazz Institute and Cultural Center 38

Federal Hill Park 32, 43

Fells Point 14, 35, 43

Fite, Henry 15

food 66-67

Fort McHenry 16, 31, 43

Goucher Mummy 59

Graffiti Alley 48

Gray, Freddie 22

Great Baltimore Fire 20

Great Depression 20

Hammond Building 19

Holiday, Billie 39

HONFest 57

Hons 5, 56-57

Horse You Came In On Saloon 83

Howard Rawlings Conservatory and Botanic Gardens 81

Inner Harbor 10-11, 21-¬

Jackson, Dr. Lillie Carroll 22

James Webb Space Telescope 21

Johns Hopkins University 21, 29, 63, 76

Jones's Town 14

Key, Francis Scott 16, 31

King, Dr. Martin Luther Jr. 23, 87

lacrosse 75

LED Art Billboard 49

Lexington Market 37

Light RailLink 43

Little Italy 32

Lovely Lane Meeting House 28

Loyola University Maryland 77

Maryland Film Festival 52

Maryland Institute College of Art 77

Maryland Science Center 44

Maryland Toleration Act 14

Maryland Zoo 80-81

Marshall, Thurgood 25

McKim, John 29

Metro Subway 42

Mr. Trash Wheel 58

Morgan State University 22, 76

Mutual United Brotherhood of Liberty 22

Nation of Islam 29

NAACP 22

National Aquarium 11

National Federation of the Blind 65

National Great Blacks in Wax Museum 45

National Road 15

Ner Israel Rabbinical College 29

Old Bay seasoning 63, 69

Old Town Friends Meeting House 17, 29

Oriole Park at Camden Yards 21, 70-71

Papermoon Diner 58

Patapsco River 6, 14

Peale, Charles Wilson 85

Peale Museum 85

Peale, Rembrandt 85

Pennsylvania Station 5

Parkway Theater 49

Paskestikweya people 13

Patterson Bowling Center 37

Phelps, Michael 61

Phoenix Shot Tower 34

Poe, Edgar Allan 24, 82, 83

Pool No. 2 49

Port Discovery Children's Museum 44

Preakness Stakes 74

Reginald F. Lewis Museum of Maryland African American History and Culture 45

Samuel D. Harris National Museum of Dentistry 47

Scott, Joyce J. 49

Sculpture Gardens at the Baltimore Museum of Art 48

Seton, St. Elizabeth Ann 29

Seven-Foot Knoll Lighthouse 10

Shakur, Tupac 39

Sherald, Amy 49

Sister Cities 90-91

Smith Island 88

Smith, Jada Pinkett 60

Sparrow's Point 19

"Star-Spangled Banner," 16, 31

Stevenson, Dr. John 14

Tubman, Harriet 25

Turnblad, Tracy 56

Underground Railroad 17

United Methodist Church 28

University of Maryland, College Park 77

US Naval Academy 86

USS Constellation 11

Walters Art Museum 51

Waring, Everett J. 22

Washington DC 16, 87

Washington Monument 4

Waters, John 56, 60

Water Taxi 43

weather 40-41

W.E.B. Dubois House 36

Westminster Burying Ground 82

Woodland people 12

World War I 20

Thanks for Visiting
BALTIMORE
Come Back Soon!